& wisdom
of
Tommy Dewar

John Dewar & Sons Ltd.
1700 London Road, Glasgow.

The Wit and Wisdom of Tommy Dewar

Copyright © John Dewar & Sons Ltd, 2001

Published by John Dewar & Sons Ltd.
1700 London Road, Glasgow G32 8XR.

All Rights Reserved. Any part of this work may be quoted for review
provided the title is credited in full.

Produced for John Dewar & Sons Ltd by The Edinburgh Consultancy.

www.EdinburghConsultancy.com

Copy: Ian Buxton   Design: Gill Waugh

Printed in the UK by St Edmundsbury Press,
Bury St Edmunds, Suffolk

ISBN
0-9540468-0-3

The Wit & Wisdom of Tommy Dewar

A selection from the speeches of Sir Thomas R. Dewar, Whisky Baron.

Sir Thomas Robert Dewar
1864 - 1930

THERE'S NO FUN LIKE WORK!

Imagine you're in your twenties, your father has just died and you've been sent to London to make vital sales for the family business. You have two 'leads' - one turns out to be bankrupt and the other is dead. What do you do?

Well, the enterprising and resourceful Thomas Dewar relied on his native wit and considerable charm. Over the years, these qualities led to considerable success in politics and business and, though he died more than seventy years ago, his wit and wisdom lives on.

Savour this selection - remember, after all, that "the only thing you can get in a hurry is trouble."

"THE LATE LORD DEWAR... WIT, HUMOURIST AND MULTI-MILLIONAIRE"

So began the obituary of Sir Thomas Robert Dewar in the *National Guardian* of 19 April 1930. Yet this describes only some of his accomplishments and says nothing of his success in politics and horse racing. Neither does it mention his assiduous art collecting nor his philanthropy.

Born in January 1864, Thomas Dewar was soon brought into the family firm, then little more than a local wine and spirit merchant. Within a short time he took charge of sales and advertising, directing his efforts initially at the English market. Over the years, in partnership with his brother John, the firm of John Dewar & Sons grew to enjoy worldwide success.

The brothers' energy and enterprise was echoed by success in other fields. Thomas Dewar was prominent in politics, being variously Sheriff of the City of London, a Conservative MP and, from 1919, an active member of the House of Lords. He trained many successful racehorses and greyhounds and his art collection included major works by Raeburn and Landseer as well as the table used by Robert Burns.

Naturally, his political career and work in the licensed trade honed his skills as a writer and speech-maker. He published several books, including *A Ramble Round the Globe*, selections from which are published here. Originally published in 1894, it was reprinted in 1904 and remains an engaging record of travel before the jet aeroplane shrank the world.

His philanthropy is still remembered in his native city. In 1924 he purchased Kinnoul Hill and gifted it to the people of Perth, together with funds to ensure its maintenance.

It remains a popular recreational area to this day.

As an after-dinner speaker, he was in great demand - urbane, witty and original. His speeches were peppered with 'Dewarisms' - sharp little epigrams of his own devising, many worthy of an Oscar Wilde or Dorothy Parker. His thoughts on business, women, the arts, and life in general illustrate a keen mind and a ready wit and it seemed to us that these Dewarisms had stood the test of time and deserved to find a wider audience.

Hence this slim volume, dedicated to the memory of a remarkable and energetic Scotsman whose name will be remembered whenever and wherever a "Dewar's" is called for.

As he said himself: "We have great regard for old age - when it is bottled!"

A Ramble Round the Globe

Tommy Dewar's story is told in his book *A Ramble Round the Globe* which was published by Chatto & Windus in 1894. Aged just 28, he set off to find new markets and in two years travelling did just that. He visited 26 countries and appointed 32 new agents - travelling by ship, stagecoach, train and New York street car. The trip cost £14,000 so, as he tells us, he watched the pennies very closely!

Back home, others were keeping an equally careful eye on expenses - the Auditor's Report of February 1895 notes "There has of late been an exceptional amount of Travelling Charges (including Colonial Journeys)..."

On Street Cars and Millionaires...

My first cab drive was what they call an 'eye-opener' to me; for although I went only a short distance, the fare was a dollar. After that, I gave up cabs, and threw in my lot with the millionaires by always using the 'street car'. Everyone uses the car, and I am not surprised at it; the fare is very moderate. Five cents will take one anywhere while cabs are very dear, and very bad.

ON BOSTON...

Now, it may not be generally known in this country, but it is well known in Boston, that there is only one place in the world, and that is Boston. Everything here is extremely proper - in fact, almost ultra-English. There are heaps of people in this headquarters of 'cult' who would much rather be found dead on Boston Common than live for ever in a double-barrelled mansion in Michigan! In fact, I have heard that when the first real Bostonian died, and went aloft, St Peter hesitated to let him through the gate; and upon the defunct one expostulating, and saying he came from Boston, St Peter remarked that that was just the difficulty.

'However,' said he, 'come in; but please don't be disappointed!' I fancy there must be a bit of satire intended somewhere in that.

On New York...

Well, my first impressions about New York were that it was a wonderful place; but I had not been there long before I came to the conclusion that the streets were about the worst I had ever seen, and I am still of this opinion. I suppose the reason is that it is such an awfully busy place, a very busy place indeed; and really everybody seems wild on the one idea - make money. I asked an American, soon after I got there, what was the use of all this rush and bustle and excitement? What came of it? Was there anything attached to it? What did men do after they had made their 'pile'?

He simply replied, 'I guess they die.'

ON CLERICAL GENTLEMEN...

We had a service on board on Sunday, when an American missionary of the Moody and Sankey type delivered a very long oration about civilising the whole world, speaking very modestly of his own countrymen, and contenting himself with saying that Americans were improved Englishmen once removed. Modesty is always beautiful, but in a clerical gentleman especially so.

The steward told me before landing that the sale of Irish whiskey had been double that of any voyage during the past twelve months, and said he accounted for it from the fact of there being six Irish priests on board!

... AND GENTLEMEN, GENERALLY

The ordeal of the Custom-House had to be gone through, and this was very trying indeed. It was terrible trouble getting through, and in my impatience while waiting I said to someone, 'Why on earth can't they have Free Trade here, and save all this bother?'
'Say, mister,' said the gentleman, 'you'd think different to that, I guess, if you made $40,000 a year through Protection like I do!'

What struck me as very strange in all this crowd was the general use of 'mister'; there was no 'sir'. It was peculiar at first, especially from the men who kept coming up saying, 'Telegraph to Europe, mister?

Telegraph to Europe?' It was different, though, when I wanted my baggage checked to the hotel, for on making inquiries about it I was told, 'This gentleman will do it for you, mister!' I saw it all then; a porter or messenger is a 'gentleman', but a common or garden passenger only a plain 'mister'!

ON PROHIBITION

I was going through a 'prohibition' State and tried to get some whisky from the conductor of the train, but without success. 'Can't do it boss; we're in a prohibition State.' However, he eventually advised me to try at a store at the next stopping place, and this I did.

'Do you sell whisky?'

'Are you sick, mister, or got a medical certificate?'

'No.'

'Then I can't do it. See, this is a prohibition State, so I can't sell it; but I reckon our cholera mixture'll about fix you. Try a bottle of that.'

I did, but to my great astonishment received a very familiar bottle which, although it was labelled on one side 'Cholera Mixture: a wine-glassful to be taken every two hours', had upon the other side the well-known label of a firm of Scotch Whisky distillers, whose name modesty requires me to suppress!

On Absinthe...

I don't think it would be quite right to pass over the smoking-room crowd without recording a word of praise to the French detachment on board. I only had one objection to them, and that was the amount of absinthe they drank!

Naturally they tried to convert us to the beauties of this stimulant; but, as far as I was concerned, I said, 'Get thee behind me, Satan! The Almighty has not given me much in the way of brains, but what little I have I will keep!'

DEWARISMS

After the success of his travel journal - it was reprinted by popular demand in 1904 - and his political career, Tommy Dewar was in great demand as a wit and after-dinner speaker. His pithy witticisms were widely reported as 'Dewarisms' and quoted in the international press.

Here follows a selection. Feel free to use them at weddings, bar mitzvahs and other social gatherings!

Some are born good,
and others make good.

Most men do not wake up to
find themselves famous; they
usually dream they are
famous, then wake up.

A man with a sense of
humour was never known
to start a revolution.

What we call confidence in ourselves we call conceit in others.

There are a great many willing to work, and a great many willing to let them

If a man upon his trade relies he must either bust or advertise.

*If you show irritation,
it is temperament.*

❧

*If others show irritation,
it is bad temper.*

❧

*If you are lavish, people say
you are a spendthrift.*

❧

*If you practise economy, you
are Scotch.*

Hope is the undergarment of optimism.

When an opinion becomes general it is generally correct.

If we are here to help others, I often wonder what the others are here for.

When a man says his word is as good as his bond, get the bond.

❧

A successful man is one who makes more than his family can spend.

❧

Talk is cheap until it gets into love letters.

Respect for old age does not extend to eggs.

The road to success is filled with women pushing their husbands along.

The cockerel does the crowing, but the hen delivers the goods.

It is a wise wife who laughs at her husband's stories. The jokes may not be funny, but some husbands are.

❧

The inventor of the bagpipes got the idea from stepping onto a cat.

❧

Sing in your bath, but first lock the door.

Do right and fear no man; don't write and fear no woman.

❧

Only women and governments are allowed to change their minds.

❧

We have a great regard for old age when it is bottled.

A night club is a place where, when the police appear at the door, the members disappear out of the window – the order of procedure being married men first.

❧

Keep advertising and advertising will keep you.

The joint stock companies often begin with a luncheon and end with a law suit.

❧

If cheerfulness counts, the bride's father is generally the best man at a wedding.

❧

The skirt of today begins anywhere and leaves off abruptly.

You cannot blame a girl who pays 30/- for a pair of silk stockings showing 28/- worth of them.

૨૭

Advertising is to business what imagination is to poetry.

૨૭

Love is an ocean of emotion entirely surrounded by expense.

If your clothes look as though you had slept in them, people are apt to think you have.

❧

Respectability is the state of never being caught doing anything which gives you pleasure.

❧

Swank – displaying the goods you wish you had.

When you hear a man say "accidents will happen" you may be pretty certain he has been doing something he ought not to have done.

❧

Never open your mouth until you are absolutely certain your brain is going to work.

*Two is company,
three is a corporation.*

*Our Poet Laureate when
visiting New York refused to
give the press reporters an
interview. The headline
in the papers next morning
was - "The King's Canary
won't chirrup".*

It is very simple to learn to live beyond your means. You mortgage your house to buy a motor, and you mortgage your motor to buy petrol.

❧

Most men are great believers in heredity until the son makes a fool of himself.

Man reaps what he sows,
unless he is an
amateur gardener.

❧

The man with a political bee
in his bonnet often gets stung.

❧

The underdog in China at the
present time appears to be
the Pekinese.

People who produce most of the trouble produce little else.

❧

We should not say "how's business", but we should say "where's business".

❧

Four-fifths of the perjury of the world is expended on tombstones, women and competitors.

It is much better to have a few hundreds in the bank than millions on the brain.

A philosopher is a man who can look at an empty glass with a smile.

In public life the hero of today is often the victim of tomorrow.

History has no record of a woman refusing diamonds — gold sometimes, but diamonds, never.

❧

The man who has nothing to do is always in a hurry.

❧

Never discuss your trouble in public — she may hear you.

Inspiration, perspiration and enthusiasm, when they are joined together in business - look out!

In church you mumble a few words and you are married; in your sleep you mumble a few words and you are divorced.

To achieve disarmament, build battleships by popular subscription.

❦

To work eight hours a day for 30/- a week is domestic service.

To work sixteen hours a day for nothing and to appear to be pleased is marriage.

The great misfortune of mankind is that only those out of office know how to solve great problems.

Some men chase women they should dodge and dodge women they should chase.

Experience is what you get while you are looking for something else.

❧

The one thing that hurts more than having to pay income tax is not having to pay income tax.

❧

Many keep poor trying to appear rich.

Money is no use until it is spent. In the case of those who do not spend it, the Government kindly assists them.

Ability without enthusiasm is like a rifle without a bullet.

There are no statues erected to men who stopped to explain their mistakes.

Think and act for yourself. When a man asks your advice it is to endorse something foolish he has already done.

🌶

Wealth is of the heart, not of the hand.

🌶

The man who knows how to make money seldom knows how to spend it.

To some mothers, life is just one darned stocking after another.

Amateur farming is a form of pursuit practised by men who have no ambition to die rich.

Hell has no terrors to a man whose love-letters have been read in court.

The only thing you can get in a hurry is trouble.

❧

Minds are like parachutes – they only function when they are open.

❧

The only popular tax is the one the other man pays.

*If you do not advertise,
you fossilise.*

*Were it not for a man's faults
he might live and die
without ever hearing his
name mentioned.*

*It is never too late for a
woman to miss an
appointment.*

There is no traffic congestion on the straight and narrow path.

Some people are always looking for a new kind of mistake to make.

Many a false step is made by standing still.

Footprints on the sands of time are not made by sitting down.

Prosperity is something which business men create to enable politicians to take all the credit.

Nothing deflates so fast as a punctured reputation.

Success is merely a matter of buying your experience cheap and selling it at a profit.

❧

If a man is not wedded to somebody, the next best thing is to be wedded to something.

❧

Optimism makes a man of 95 buy a new suit of clothes and two pairs of trousers.

Clothes might not make a man, but well-cut clothes keep some men out of prison.

❧

Where there is a will you often get a law suit.

❧

If we had not so many bad people in the world we should not have so many good lawyers.

A man who can laugh at his own misfortune is an asset to the community.

৵

There is no fun like work.

৵

Do nothing, be nothing, say nothing and you will avoid criticism.

No man is a hero to his mother-in-law.

No place is so lonely as London when one hasn't a friend.

Fish stimulates the brain, but fishing stimulates the imagination.

A man who can borrow money easily never wants it badly.

🐌

I always like to be temperate when touching the spirit of temperance.

🐌

There are many reformers who would like to exploit their ideas with other people's money.

If you forbid a man to do a thing, you will add the joy of piracy and the zest of smuggling to his life.

Some men are born great; others have corpulency thrust upon them.

Man forgets, woman forgives, and the world remembers.

Golfers hit little balls at intervals and talk about them the rest of their lives.

❦

The less a man has to say the more words he uses in saying it.

❦

It may be dangerous to make love to a man's wife, but it is safer than making love to his widow.

An ounce of flattery is worth more than a ton of obituary.

The surest way to be happy is to get so busy that you have no time to be unhappy.

Refinement is the ability to yawn without opening one's mouth.

A good wife always asks her husband's advice when she has decided what to do.

❧

Poets are born and not paid.

❧

If the good die young, what a lot of old reprobates there must be in this world.

Don't question your wife's judgement. Look who she married.

Few of us can examine our family tree without finding some queer birds in the branches.

Never invest in a going concern until you know which way it is going.

🐦

Of two evils choose the more interesting.

🐦

The greatest mistake you can make in this life is to be continually fearing you will make one.

*Life may be difficult,
but it's the only thing
worth living.*

Thomas R. Dewar.